BIGGEST NAMES IN SPORTS
CODY BELLINGER
BASEBALL STAR

by Connor Stratton

T0010138

FOCUS
READERS®

NAVIGATOR

WWW.FOCUSREADERS.COM

Focus Readers is distributed by North Star Editions:
sales@northstareditions.com | 888-417-0195

Produced for Focus Readers by Red Line Editorial.

Photographs ©: Sam Gangwer/AP Images, cover, 1; Matt Slocum/AP Images, 4–5; Mark J. Terrill/AP Images, 7, 19, 22–23; Charlie Riedel/AP Images, 9; Jim McIsaac/Getty Images Sport/Getty Images, 10–11; Larry Goren/Four Seam Images/AP Images, 13; Michael Spomer/Cal Sport Media/AP Images, 15; Marcio Jose Sanchez/AP Images, 16–17, 27; Charles Krupa/AP Images, 21; Brian Rothmuller/Icon Sportswire/AP Images, 25; Red Line Editorial, 29

Library of Congress Cataloging-in-Publication Data
Names: Stratton, Connor, author.
Title: Cody Bellinger : baseball star / by Connor Stratton.
Description: Lake Elmo, MN : Focus Readers, [2021] | Series: Biggest names
   in sports | Includes index. | Audience: Grades 4-6
Identifiers: LCCN 2020039043 (print) | LCCN 2020039044 (ebook) | ISBN
   9781644936979 (hardcover) | ISBN 9781644937334 (paperback) | ISBN
   9781644938058 (pdf) | ISBN 9781644937693 (ebook)
Subjects: LCSH: Bellinger, Cody, 1995---Juvenile literature. | Outfielders
   (Baseball)--United States--Biography--Juvenile literature. | Baseball
   players--United States--Biography--Juvenile literature. | Los Angeles
   Dodgers (Baseball team)--History--Juvenile literature. | Most Valuable
   Player Award (Baseball)--History--Juvenile literature.
Classification: LCC GV865.B346 S77 2021 (print) | LCC GV865.B346 (ebook)
   | DDC 796.357092 [B]--dc23
LC record available at https://lccn.loc.gov/2020039043
LC ebook record available at https://lccn.loc.gov/2020039044

Printed in the United States of America
Mankato, MN
012021

ABOUT THE AUTHOR

Connor Stratton writes and edits children's books. Raised just outside the Windy City, he loves all things Bears, Cubs, Blackhawks, and Bulls. He was unlucky enough to attend the ill-fated Bartman game in 2003, and he was glad when the 2016 team laid the Cubs' curse to rest. He lives in Minnesota.

TABLE OF CONTENTS

CHAPTER 1

PLAYOFF WALK-OFF

Cody Bellinger stared down the Milwaukee Brewers pitcher. Bellinger was one swing away from winning the game for the Los Angeles Dodgers. It was Game 4 of the 2018 National League Championship Series (NLCS). The game was tied 1–1 in the bottom of the 13th inning. Bellinger's teammate

Bellinger cranks out a game-winning hit during the 2018 National League Championship Series.

5

Manny Machado stood on first base. The Dodgers had two outs.

The Brewers pitcher threw toward the plate. The ball hit the dirt and bounced away from the catcher. It was a **wild pitch**. Machado easily advanced to second base. That changed everything. Machado was now in **scoring position**.

After several pitches, Bellinger had a full count. The next pitch hung over the inside corner of the plate. Bellinger cracked a hard ground ball past the first baseman. Machado rounded third and sprinted toward home plate. The Brewers' right fielder threw a laser to the catcher. It was a nearly perfect throw, but Machado

Manny Machado (8) celebrates after scoring the winning run in Game 4 of the 2018 NLCS.

was too fast. He slid behind the catcher to score the winning run. Bellinger had hit his first career **walk-off**. More importantly, he had helped the Dodgers tie the series at two games apiece.

Los Angeles won again in Game 5, but Milwaukee took Game 6. In Game 7, the Brewers scored in the first inning to take a quick lead. But Bellinger didn't let that lead last. He stepped up to the plate in the second inning with a runner on first. Bellinger swung at a fastball right down the middle. His bat connected perfectly and launched the ball out of the park. The go-ahead home run soared all the way to the upper deck.

The Dodgers never gave up their lead. They scored three more runs in the sixth and won the game 5–1. But Bellinger's two-run homer was all they ended up needing. Because of his incredible

Bellinger crushes a two-run homer in Game 7 of the 2018 NLCS.

play, Bellinger became the NLCS Most Valuable Player (MVP).

Unfortunately for Dodgers fans, Los Angeles didn't come through in the World Series. They lost to the Boston Red Sox in five games. Even so, Bellinger had proved he was one of the best players in baseball.

CHAPTER 2

LIKE FATHER, LIKE SON

Cody Bellinger was born in Scottsdale, Arizona, on July 13, 1995. Cody grew up surrounded by baseball. His father, Clay, played in Major League Baseball (MLB). Clay spent three seasons with the New York Yankees and one with the Anaheim Angels. In those four seasons, he took home three World Series rings.

Cody and his dad take part in a Little League World Series game in 2007.

Cody's dad played his last major league game in 2002. But he was still able to help Cody learn the game. They worked on Cody's swing at the batting cages. Cody's dad also coached Cody's teams. And in 2007, Cody's team made it to the Little League World Series. He showed his skills on national TV.

A TASTE OF THE BIG LEAGUES

With a father in MLB, Cody saw what life was like for the pros. He experienced that life himself at the Little League World Series. Cody played in front of news cameras and thousands of fans. He talked to reporters on national TV. For his teammates, the series was the closest they would get to the big leagues. For Cody, it was just the beginning.

Cody takes a swing during a 2012 game for top high school players.

Cody continued to improve his game in high school. He hit .429 his senior year. At first, Cody planned to play college ball before trying for the pros. But his plans changed in June 2013. The Dodgers selected Cody in the fourth round of the MLB **Draft**. The opportunity was too good to pass up. Cody was thrilled, but he hadn't made it to the majors yet. First he would have to prove himself in the minor leagues.

After two years in the minors, Cody found his stride. He'd been solid at the plate, but he hadn't hit many home runs. Then Cody changed his batting stance. He stopped holding his bat upright. Instead, he held the bat flat and wiggled his wrists before swinging. Those changes kept Cody loose and gave him more power.

Cody covers first base during a 2016 game with the
Oklahoma City Dodgers.

His work paid off. Cody started hitting
homer after homer. He was also selected
as an All-Star in 2015 and 2016. The
bright lights of Dodger Stadium were
finally in sight.

CHAPTER 3

ROOKIE OF THE YEAR

In April 2017, Cody Bellinger played in his first big-league game. In the ninth inning, the 21-year-old **rookie** swung for the fences. He hit a choppy ground ball instead. Bellinger **hustled** to first base for an infield single. It wasn't pretty, but he'd gotten his first major league hit.

Bellinger hits a single in his first major league game.

17

Bellinger quickly showed he could do more than just hustle. He belted two homers in his fifth major league game. Then, on June 19, Bellinger launched the 20th and 21st home runs of his career. He became the fastest player in MLB history to hit 21 career home runs.

BASEBALL BROTHERS

The Bellinger family had a lot to celebrate in 2017. Cody was playing in his first season with the Dodgers. That same year, Cody's younger brother, Cole, was drafted by the San Diego Padres. Like Cody, Cole went to the minors straight out of high school. Unlike his brother, Cole is a pitcher. He hoped to pitch against Cody in the majors someday.

Bellinger admires a home run during a 2017 game against the Pittsburgh Pirates.

Even better, Bellinger was in great company. The 2017 Dodgers featured incredible hitting, pitching, and **depth**. The team finished the regular season with the best record in the league. Bellinger played a huge role. He hit 39 home runs. That was a National League rookie record.

Nobody was surprised when he became the 2017 Rookie of the Year.

In October, the Dodgers reached their first World Series in 29 years. But the Dodgers lost to the Houston Astros in a heartbreaking seven-game series. Bellinger struggled in the series. He struck out a record-setting 29 times in the **postseason**.

The sting of the World Series defeat lasted into the 2018 season. Through July, Bellinger batted just .237. However, he picked things back up in August. He also showed strength in other ways, including defense. He proved to be strong at both first base and center field.

Bellinger makes a spectacular catch to rob the Boston Red Sox of a hit in the 2018 World Series.

The Dodgers won their division again. But they lost in the World Series for the second year in a row. Los Angeles fans licked their wounds and looked ahead to 2019. Meanwhile, Bellinger worked hard to push his game to the next level.

CHAPTER 4

MOST VALUABLE PLAYER

Going into the 2019 season, Cody Bellinger knew he could improve. He decided to change his swing again. Bellinger worked with hitting experts. They watched videos of Bellinger's at-bats. They even created 3D maps of his swing. These maps helped the experts

Bellinger follows through on a swing during a 2019 game against the Arizona Diamondbacks.

learn how Bellinger's body best created power.

Bellinger started holding his bat more upright. He also held his hands higher. These changes made Bellinger more comfortable at the plate. That way, he could focus better on each pitch.

The results were immediate. In 2019, Bellinger struck out much less often. And one month into the season, he led MLB in nearly every batting category. Bellinger finished the season strong as well. He batted .305 and cranked out 47 homers.

Bellinger's skills shone on the field, too. He made just two **errors** the entire season in right field. And he wowed fans

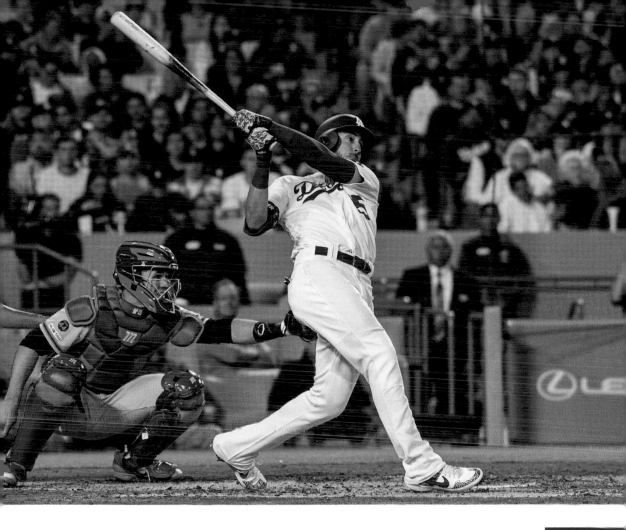

Bellinger launches a grand slam against the San Francisco Giants in 2019.

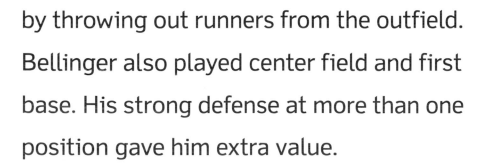

by throwing out runners from the outfield. Bellinger also played center field and first base. His strong defense at more than one position gave him extra value.

With Bellinger's help, Los Angeles won 106 games in 2019. That was the most wins in team history. Meanwhile, Bellinger was the clear choice for the National League's MVP. However, the Dodgers lost in the 2019 playoffs.

OUTFIELD DOUBLE PLAY

Bellinger showed off his arm in a 2019 game against the New York Mets. With the bases loaded, a Mets batter hit a fly ball to right field. Bellinger caught the ball to put the batter out. Then he threw the ball 300 feet (91 m) to nail a runner at third base. It was an amazing double play. During Bellinger's next at-bat, the fans at Dodger Stadium roared with chants of "MVP!"

Bellinger swings for the fences during a game against the Los Angeles Angels in 2020.

In 2020, the Dodgers won their division for the eighth year in a row. In the NLCS, the Atlanta Braves forced Los Angeles to a seven-game series. Bellinger came up big. He hit the game-winning home run to send the Dodgers to the World Series. Then they defeated the Tampa Bay Rays to win it all. Bellinger was a champion at last!

CODY BELLINGER

- Height: 6 feet 4 inches (193 cm)
- Weight: 203 pounds (92 kg)
- Birth date: July 13, 1995
- Birthplace: Scottsdale, Arizona
- High school: Hamilton High School (Chandler, Arizona)
- Minor league teams: Arizona League Dodgers (2013–2014); Ogden Raptors (2014); Rancho Cucamonga Quakes (2015); Tulsa Drillers (2016); Oklahoma City Dodgers (2016–2017)
- MLB team: Los Angeles Dodgers (2017–)
- Major awards: National League Rookie of the Year (2017); National League All-Star (2017, 2019); NLCS MVP (2018); National League MVP (2019); Silver Slugger Award (2019); Gold Glove Award (2019); World Series champion (2020)

Ogden

Los Angeles

Rancho Cucamonga

Tulsa

Chandler

Oklahoma City

Scottsdale

FOCUS ON
CODY BELLINGER

Write your answers on a separate piece of paper.

1. Write a paragraph explaining the main ideas of Chapter 4.

2. Do you think Bellinger has been more valuable to the Dodgers on offense or defense? Why?

3. In which season did Bellinger hit 47 home runs?

> **A.** 2017
> **B.** 2018
> **C.** 2019

4. What advantage did Cody have when he was growing up?

> **A.** He was always a home-run hitter.
> **B.** He was coached by his dad, who had played in MLB.
> **C.** He knew he would have time to develop his skills in college.

Answer key on page 32.

GLOSSARY

depth
Having many talented players on a team.

draft
A system that allows teams to acquire new players coming into a league.

errors
Mistakes by a player who should have been able to get an out or stop a runner from advancing.

hustled
Moved quickly and gave a full effort.

postseason
A set of games played after the regular season to decide which team will be the champion.

rookie
A professional athlete in his or her first year.

scoring position
When a player is on second or third base. From this position, a base hit will usually allow the runner to score.

walk-off
A hit that scores a run to immediately win the game.

wild pitch
A pitch that is off target and not caught by the catcher.

TO LEARN MORE

BOOKS

Fishman, Jon M. *Cody Bellinger.* Minneapolis: Lerner Publications, 2021.

Frederick, Jace. *Baseball's New Wave: The Young Superstars Taking Over the Game.* Mendota Heights, MN: Press Room Editions, 2019.

Ventura, Marne. *STEM in Baseball.* Minneapolis: Abdo Publishing, 2018.

NOTE TO EDUCATORS

Visit **www.focusreaders.com** to find lesson plans, activities, links, and other resources related to this title.

INDEX

Answer Key: 1. Answers will vary; **2.** Answers will vary; **3.** C; **4.** B